# DENISE COCHRAN

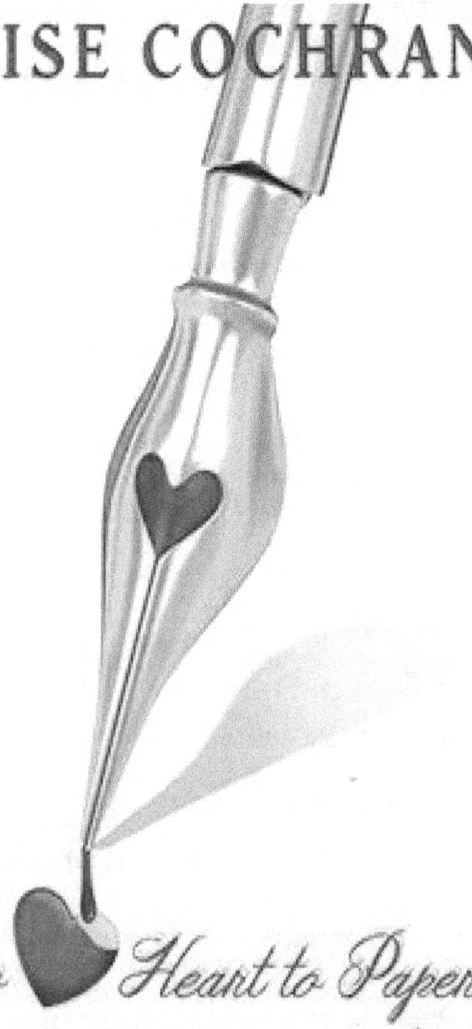

*Pen to Heart to Paper*

## My Book of Inspirations

*FIRST EDITION*

Pen to Heart ~ Heart to Paper is a registered copyright.

ISBN: 978-1530180356

Live with Purpose (LWP3)

*Clarice L. Johnson – Senior Editor and Publisher*
*C. J. Loray Productions, Inc.*
*St. Clair Shores, Michigan*

*L'Oreal Hartwell – Cover Design*
*The HMG Agency*
*Saginaw, Michigan*

# <u>Dedication</u>

This book is dedicated to my loving mother, Earline Cochran.

You are more than the wind beneath my wings, you are the light that guides me through darkness. You are more than a shoulder to cry on, you are the soother of all my discomfort. Thank you for encouraging me, for supporting me and for believing in me. No matter what journey I decide to take, you stand by my side proudly. I am grateful for you. I honor you. I love you!

-Your Daughter, Denise

Pen to heart, heart to paper...that's how I create my personal masterpieces.

I am grateful for being able to share the meditations of my heart with you. I hope that these words warm your heart and bring comfort as you nourish your mind and your spirit.

I compose these written symphonies, pen to heart, heart to paper.

- Denise Cochran

Discipline is the key to focusing
your mind.
Determination is what drives
your discipline.
Desire is obtained when you apply discipline
and determination.

Perception is the way you view things, your thoughts, your opinion of something.

What is your perception of you? What is your perception of where your life is?

Take a moment, are you satisfied with what YOU think about you and your life?

The only person who can change your perception of you, is you!

Know your worth.

Don't allow others to taint your

opinion of yourself.

Don't seek approval from others

about your destiny.

Don't become engaged in things that

waste time and effort.

Don't get lost in someone else's dream.

Don't stop believing that you

are of greatness.

Don't open doors that should

remain closed.

Don't prolong your abundant life searching

for your value.

Know your worth.

Peace is found, when reality is accepted.

Your current situation is the result of your past decisions.

If you are not satisfied, the future is your canvas.

Create your masterpiece.

Ownership of the leader in you, brings

ownership of your success.

Life consists of choices:

1. Live in your purpose, or

2. Live unfulfilled

Choose wisely

We have to continuously recondition our minds. We were born to be great! Let's speak, act and live in the greatness that God purposed for our lives. Change your way of thinking and speaking. Always identify and walk away with something POSITIVE from every potentially negative situation. Surround yourself with positive influence and COMPLETELY rid your life of negative things, thoughts and people. The path to renewal is lonely, but very necessary. You may lose a lot of family and friends along the way, but be receptive and grateful for the new positive relationships you will gain.

Live by belief in a higher power.

Live by belief that you reap what you sow.

Live by belief in the fruit of the spirit.

Live by belief that to love is Godly.

Live by belief that there is a purpose for your life.

Dream means to contemplate the

possibility of doing something.

Or, a strongly desired goal or purpose.

Don't be afraid to dream.

Don't allow someone else's definition of a

dream, be defining of your limit.

For a dream removed limits.

A dream opened doors.

A dream made history.

A dream allowed many of our brothers and

sisters to be proudly introduced as, "The

First Black or African-American to..."

What is your dream?

I am changing, evolving, growing, accepting and forgiving a lot of things about me and my past. I can't correct all the mistakes or mend all the hurt I may have caused. But, I will right the wrongs that are in my control and continue to make better choices.

These are Denise's first steps to recovering.

Tell yourself you are the originator of all

things positive in your life.

Believe what you said.

When you KNOW there is a purpose for
your life, there's a yearning
deep within you.
It's a feeling of burning fire inside you and
the only way to extinguish the
fire is to release it.
I challenge you today to release the fire and
release the desire within you!
Live with Purpose!

We all have situations and circumstances.

But, we have to be, and stay, receptive in

order to receive the lesson in each trial.

When God is using us, we can't question or

choose the situation that best suits us.

He knows the outcome from the very start.

It is our responsibility, in God's Army, to

have faith and move forward in battle,

trusting and knowing we have already won!

Followers don't lead winners.

Leaders don't follow losers.

You are in your change.

God doesn't give a timeframe on transformation.

He has no deadline to meet.

Patience, perseverance, productivity and power is part of your change.

Embrace it.

Shelter means to protect from
harm or danger.
Do we seek protection from the
elements of this world?
Do we seek shelter from the things that
have caused us danger?
Do we seek or find comfort where safety
and security is promised to us?
Do we understand that shelter is not only a
physical place of protection, but shelter can
also be a spiritual place of protection?
I know where we can find protection
against all the things that
can cause us harm.
I know the provider of the highest level of
security against the spiritual and physical
enemies of this world.
I invite you to seek shelter with the only
protector who will watch over you forever.
I encourage you to seek divine safeguard for
your life, and for the lives of your family.
I ask of you, seek shelter.
Seek God.

An open mind is God's pathway
to your thinking.
An open heart is God's pathway
to your spirit.
Remain an open vessel and watch God
change your life.

Let go of fear.

Let go of doubt.

Let go of negative energy.

Let go of negative thoughts.

Let go of negative speaking.

Let go of negative self-talk.

Let go of negative people.

Let go of negative situations.

Let go of negative influences.

Let go of negative habits.

Let go of procrastination.

Let go of hindrance.

Let go.

Focus on who you are, not what you have, because who you are is the real treasure.

Growth is when you recognize that the things you've experienced and endured in life wasn't just for teaching you, but was meant to inspire and help change the life of someone else.

Growth is when criticism is embraced as a tool and a checklist for improvement, not internalized as judgement and jealousy.

Growth is when you have learned how to truly forgive someone, and no longer have a need or desire to remind them that you won't forget.

Faith is powerful.  It is built on that which you cannot see or touch, but has the ability to change circumstances and move mountains.

Today is your day of confidence,

determination and accomplishment.

There are no goals too high

for you to reach.

Success resides in you.

Unlock the doors of opportunity.

Think it! Say it! Do it!

On your mark!

Get set!

Go!

When you think and dwell in lack,

you live in lack.

When you verbalize the negative, I can't, I

don't, I won't, you introduce your mind to

lack and your actions will soon follow.

Our words hold power!

We need to be mindful of the things we

think and speak into our lives.

This is a new beginning. Let's thrive to finish

as powerfully, productive and

prosperous as we start it!

You are the epitome of strength for many!

You bare gifts that exceed

your own expectation!

You are the achiever of all that God

has put before you!

You are phenomenal!

You got this!

Repetitively, do the thing that you are good at, and you will begin to effortlessly walk in your purpose.

Purpose is God's blueprint for

your life, your destiny.

Power is what God graced you with to

control the direction of your life.

Passion is the gift God gave you to become

intimate with your Purpose

and your Power.

Live with Purpose.

Live with Power.

Live with Passion.

Give advice as if you were

looking in a mirror.

Changing your mindset, launches you
into unknown territory.
Changing your mindset, allows you to
explore, rather than fear,
the unknown territory.
Changing your mindset, makes you a
conqueror of, rather than being defeated
by, the unknown territory.

Have you thought about it?

Have you asked God for it?

Have you prepared yourself for it?

Have you opened up to receive it?

Have you opened your mind, and your eyes,

to recognize it?

Have you asked yourself what

you will do with it?

Have you braced yourself to accept

everything that comes with it?

When you ask for it, be ready.

God doesn't use your calendar.

He sets His own dates.

Let your life be an inspiration to others.

Give of yourself and your time freely.

Speak positive proclamations into your life.

Teach your family to think

and speak positively.

Change your mind, change your life.

You were introduced to me when you were

young, sweet and innocent.

You opened your heart to me,

because I was "the one."

You trusted me, because you believed that I

would never hurt you.

You cried for me, because I couldn't

make you happy.

You rejected me, because you feared being

disappointed again.

You allowed me to return to you, because

you can't live without me.

Hello...my name is LOVE.

Mix, Purging and Preparing. Add

Productivity. Stir in Peace.

Serve as Prosperity.

This is my recipe for new life.

Stand firm in who you are!

Let no man's opinion of who you are, be the guiding force in your life.

Do not give energy to the negativity generated by the people who are intimidated by and uncomfortable with your level of intelligence.

God made you a warrior!

Stand firm in who you are!

The negative company you keep is not the only thing of which you should be cautious. Your negative thoughts could be your most dangerous toxin.

Are we so brain washed that we don't

recognize that we are born of superiority?

Are we so consumed with how society says

we should live, that we confine ourselves?

Are we so unsure of who we are,

that we are blinded of our own

strength and power?

Are we trapped by the rules that others

have laid out for our success?

Are we limited by our own

feelings of inadequacy?

Negativity is a learned behavior and we've had years of practice.
Let's challenge ourselves to change, for positivity is also a learned behavior.
We know what negativity does and how it impacts our lives.
Let's explore and relish in the impact positivity has on the remainder of our lives!
Think positively.
Speak positively.
Live positively!

The lives you touch leaves an impact.
Decide whether your impact is positive or
negative.

Spiritual growth is reflective and rewarded.

When you are being purged by God, there's

a change that happens on the inside.

And in His time, becomes reflective

on the outside.

That is the reward.

Your time for success was already

established, already written.

Your experiences had to be laid out and

orchestrated just right.

Your acceptance of your choices and your

outcomes had to be impressed

upon our heart.

Your life is now being purged and

positioned for that time that

was already written.

Believe that there is no power

greater than God.

Believe that there is no such thing as too

much for Him to handle.

Believe that there is no such thing as failure,

when standing securely in His Word.

Believe that there is truth in His promises.

Believe that there is healing in His hands.

Believe that there is a lesson in

His unconditional love.

Believe that there is grace and mercy in

His forgiveness.

Believe that there is no power

greater the God.

Hope is the expectancy your heart feels
when you are on the verge of
something good.

Accept that your mind is creative.

Allow the images of your dreams

to come true.

Believe that there is nothing you can't do.

Plan to pursue what your heart desires.

Live in the outcome of all your hard work.

God will continue opening doors.

When He has closed a door, leave it shut!

We are our biggest interference.

Recognize your POTENTIAL.

Understand your PURPOSE.

Prepare to PERSEVERE.

Be PERSISTENT.

Live in PROSPERITY.

The wealthy became wealthy, because they

always believed they were rich.

Inspire yourself with this today:

I know God has placed me where I'm

supposed to be at this very moment.

It's my time. I've been in this same place

before and backed up and backed out.

Not today. Not anymore!

This is my time! I am a warrior!

I am a winner! I am wealthy,

in ALL aspects of my life!

Sometimes we have to step back to

recognize a blessing.

We get caught up in the package and not

the delivery.

Live in your truth.

Live in your reality.

Live in positivity.

Love yourself first.

Love others genuinely.

Love unselfishly.

Laugh at yourself.

Laugh from deep within.

Laugh often.

Words are nourishment for the

mind, spirit and soul.

They cost nothing and have infinite value.

Vision is a preview to the soul.

It gives a compendious perspective (concise view) of what is embedded in the heart.

Vision is the inception of your inner belief system.

Once you conceive that you can achieve whatever you have proclivity (desire) for, your vision becomes your reality.

STOP! Don't spend another moment of your life wondering what could have been.

STOP! Don't believe that you can't have or be what you desire or deserve.

STOP! Don't envy those who are doing what you've always wanted to do.

STOP! Don't allow limits to become the dwelling place of your dreams.

STOP! Now GO get your abundant life!

Faith is not about "what" you believe in, it's about "who" you believe in. Remain faithful to God and your life will change.

Words are the mirror to what's in your

heart.  What does your heart reflect?

Be careful to whom or what you expose

your energy.

It's simple math:

Two like signs become a positive sign.

Two unlike signs become a negative sign.

Change the words you feed into your mind.

You are your biggest mental influence.

Speak positivity and life into yourself.

Your heart is the flashlight to your love.

It shines light on the pathway to happiness,

joy, peace and longevity.

Living in mediocracy was never

intended for our lives.

We were born to be of opulence

and to live in abundance.

We have to unravel our tangled web of

understanding, and transform our thinking

into believers, into achievers, into receivers.

We are exceptional.

We are magnificent.

We are leaders.

Change is not meant to be easy.

Change is meant to be endured.

It is yours, give thanks.

It gives you purpose, show gratitude.

It allows you to try again, give praise.

Its value never decreases, give honor.

Give God the Glory for the Gift of Life.

In life, in order to elevate your mind, your circumstance, your spirit, your relationship with God, you have to isolate and evaluate.

Live.

Live with purpose, knowing that life is a
priceless gift hand-wrapped by God.

Love.

Love like a little child or as if it is your first
time, pure, unadulterated and
unconditional.

Laugh.

Laugh from a place deep down inside, as if
laughter is the only language you know.

Show understanding in a place of confusion.

Be kind in a place of harshness.

Be forgiving in a place of transgression.

How can you expect your heart to heal, if
you continue to allow the
thing or the person
that broke it to have endless access to it?

Give the benefit of your experience to those who think they walk alone.

In order to grow, you must plant the seed,

fertilize the soil and water daily.

Which means:

In order to grow, you must choose God,

study the Word and daily apply

what you learn.

In life, we typically follow the pattern set by society.

We go above and beyond to be the best by their standard, in order to receive awards and accolades for our achievement.

But, what greater reward is there than to serve a God whose only prerequisite is serve and love Him.

He only asks that we give Him glory and honor in order to receive the most priceless reward of all, eternal life!

Speak your words as inspiration,
not as confrontation.

When you trust in a higher power, there is

no room for doubt.

When you have faith, there is

no room for fear.

When you believe that there is purpose for

your life, there is no room for mediocracy.

Every aspect of your life has a purpose and

breakthrough comes in due season.

Winter doesn't come before Fall.

Summer doesn't come before Spring.

The seasons change in the order God has

directed, for transitioning,

for harvest, for growth.

Your life is like a season,

changing in divine order.

The power of purging provides a profound peace that personifies the process of purifying your life.

Just when you prepare to

send out invitations

to your "Pity Party,"

God sends His Heavenly Messengers

(Angels) to crash the party.

Stop settling down with people who don't share your vision and passion. Stop allowing people in your life who have no desire to back you or push you to your success. Dedication, loyalty, support. If they don't show these qualities, let them go. God has your army already hand-picked. Let Him prepare you, WARRIOR!

Your one experience, may be someone else's lifetime.

True self-examination is hurtful, revealing,

offensive, agonizing, resentful,

shocking, and devastating.

True self-examination is truthful,

unadulterated (pure), refining, renewing,

unbiased, clarifying, purifying and healthy.

But, most importantly, necessary!

Brave life's waves.

Weather life's storms.

Win life's game.

When making change in your life, you tend

to get caught up in the pain.

The pain of past bad decisions.

The pain of past losses.

The pain of past hurt.

The pain of past friendships.

The pain of past relationships.

The pain of past transgressions.

When you change, accept that it is just that,

your past and you were the author.

Learn from it, grow from it, teach from it.

Now prepare for a powerful future, you are

still the author!

Joy is not something that can be stolen, if it is locked down on the inside of you.

You have to learn to love from a distance,

but the key to that is, YOU have to be okay

with it. Until you sit down and stop chasing

love from people who only take, because

you give, only then will you allow love to

come in and show you how it really feels.

Love doesn't mean you have to run

yourself into the ground.

Love is not supposed to hurt in order

to show proof of it.

Love is a reflection of what is in your heart.

Love should be a joy to share,

not a burden to bare.

Family is the most sacred relationship you can have. When you put love, time, morals, guidance, sacrifice and support into raising your family, you get to reap the benefit of knowing that it all pays off in the end.

Is it you?

Is it you, that keeps yourself

from spiritual growth?

Is it you, that sabotages your

present and future?

Is it you, that won't allow you to dig into

your depth of creativity, wisdom

and knowledge?

Is it you, that keeps track of your failure?

Is it you, that hinders your

success and prosperity?

Is it you, that does not know

how to forgive you?

Is it you, that does not know

how to love you?

Before you sit and ponder, searching for all

the many reasons why it could be someone

else, ask yourself, simply, is it you?

The "Force" Awakens

When God does His work of cleansing,

restoring and renewing you on the "inside,"

nothing can penetrate you on the "outside."

When God does His work of purging,

purifying and preparing you on the "inside"

nothing can prevail over

you on the "outside."

When God, who is "The Force," awakens His

Spirit in you to strengthen and transform

you, the enemy can't weaken you, can't

defeat you and can't destroy you.

Use your words to lift up in elevation, not to put down in degradation.

A dead end, a two lane highway (constantly back and forth) or an open road... which describes your life?

You are the creator of your own dream.

You are the writer of your own story.

You are the decision maker

for your own life.

You are the director of your own steps.

You are the controller

of your own outcomes.

You are the voice of

your own encouragement.

You are the traveler of your own journey.

You are the leader of your own tribe.

You are the giver of your own gifts.

You are the receiver of your own blessings.

You are the person God

purposed you to be,

live your own life with no question,

regret or comparison.

Love the person who doesn't know how to give or receive love.
You will be giving a valuable lesson that will last a lifetime.

There's a drive inside of you that moves you
to do things outside of the normal.
There's a moment of unrest that you
experience as you move in this direction of
which you've always dreamed.
There's a feeling of being unsure as you
take on this big task, not knowing the
outcome, but you take it anyway.
There's a confidence in you that you've
never had before, as you step proudly into
unknown territory.
There's this thing you possess, you only
need to have a small amount of it.
It has no monetary worth, but it has infinite
value and can move mountains.
It's called Faith!

Live with Purpose.

Live with Power.

Live with Passion.

Find the therapy in sharing your experience.
It heals you from your past and gives hope
to the person living in it right now.

Reconnect with yourself.

Reconnect with God.

Reconnect with your mind.

Reconnect with your spirit.

Reconnect with your body.

Reconnect with your heart.

Reconnect with your love.

Reconnect with your truth.

Reconnect with your trust.

Reconnect with your loyalty.

Reconnect with your integrity.

Reconnect with your moral value.

Reconnect with your gifts.

Reconnect with your time.

Reconnect with your family.

Reconnect with your money.

When you unplug and reconnect,

the power is restored.

Reconnect! Reconnect! Reconnect!

Follow the directions precisely.

You will never get lost.

We can learn so much from

our little children.

They live in the moment,

like there's no tomorrow.

They love like it's the greatest thing

they've ever known.

They laugh so genuinely and heartfelt,

it's contagious.

Take lessons from the children.

They have a lifetime of learning

ahead of them.

But, they innocently teach us some of the

core values many have forgotten

in their own lifetime.

Live with Purpose.

Know that you are a gift from the Most High. Your talent is what you possess and is tailored to who you are. Your talent is just as distinct as your fingerprint, there are no two alike. Sometimes you may have to dig a little deeper to discover it, or you may have to simply stop ignoring it. Talent is natural, you're born with it. Talent is not learned, it is perfected.

When you Live with Purpose, you begin to Live On Purpose.

Live with Purpose. Live with Power. Live with Passion. (LWP3)

Always remember that Jesus was a gift to us from God! He loved us enough to share His Son with us! On this day and every day, not only remember the birth of Christ, but reflect on what it means to give unselfishly. Because not only did God allow him to be born in the flesh, Jesus also died for our sins! What a superb example by God and His Son, of unselfish love!

Stay focused on finding your way.

Sometimes we get lost in this

thing called life.

We can sometimes lose sight of the goals

and the direction we have set for our lives.

We tend to get side-tracked by distractions

that come in all forms, be it family,

finance, work or health.

We must find a way to stay focused, and

not lose sight of our vision.

Take a moment each day and remind

yourself of your goals, whether

long or short-term.

Love, embrace and live in the gift you are given, and it will bring you infinite wealth and prosperity.

Allow purpose to be your motivating force

for change, for building,

for empowering, for success.

Allow truth to be the guide for setting and

obtaining realistic goals.

Allow belief in who you are to be the

foundation for your confidence and ability

to seek what your heart desires.

Allow determination to drive you to

"complete" everything you start.

Allow a receptive mind and spirit to take

you where your life was destined to be.

Storms will come and go.

It's your preparation, planning and actions
that help you weather the storm.

Spend time opening your heart and your mind to self-examination, self-evaluation and self-improvement. There won't be time left to examine and evaluate the shortcomings of someone else.

The power of positive thinking can and will drive you to positive action.
Have confidence in your ability to turn your negative circumstance into a positive accomplishment.

To simply give love the way you want to receive love, could start a new trend.

In order to LEARN, we must be TAUGHT.
In order to ACHIEVE,
we must APPLY the lesson.
In school, the instructor puts together
what's called a lesson plan, developed to
guide learning in a structured manner.
As we absorb this lesson and upon
mastering each grade level, we are
advanced to the next grade
until we "graduate."
Some graduate with honors, some by the
skin of their teeth and then
some don't graduate at all.
In life, in spirituality, in success, are you an
honor student, a mediocre student
or a dropout?

True friendship is the forgotten gem.

Not only is it priceless, but no matter how

much it goes through,

True friendship cannot be tarnished.

Live with Purpose.

Live with Power.

Live with Passion.

Realize Your Truth.

Recognize Your Growth.

Release Your Strength.

Choose Your Canvas.

Claim Your Place.

Create Your Masterpiece.

Failed vision only comes to the unfocused.

Failed power only comes by lack of energy.

Failed goals only comes
by lack of completion.

Failed knowledge only comes
by lack of comprehending.

Failed faith only comes to the unbeliever.

Failed progress only comes to the stagnant.

Failed life only comes to
the negative thinker.

Don't fail.

Put your best foot forward

and let go of fear.

Have confidence in your ideas

and don't be discouraged.

Know that your best exceeds others

expectations of you.

Know that your worst exceeds others

expectations of you.

Keep your eyes focused on your goals and

never underestimate your power.

Speak life into every aspect of your life and

your dream.

In order to have a new life, you have to let go of the old one. You get attached to friends, relationships, lifestyles, jobs, habits, material things and even some family. Every relationship or encounter is not always healthy. You have to understand that when you thrive to become a new you, a different you, you can't take the toxic people, things or situations with you.

Growth is about release. Release of the things that hinder, stunt or stop growth. Release of the things that do not promote positivity, productivity, progress or prosperity. In order to change your life, you have to be "willing" to let go of the toxins.

Never base the change in your life on the

expectations of others.

No one expected you to change.

Live in Expectation of the things that you
are worthy to receive.
Live in Expectation of the reward for your
diligence and endurance.
Live in Expectation of the gratification for
accomplishing your goals.
Live in Expectation that belief in God will
change the direction of your life.
Live in Expectation of the blessings for
which you pray and ask God.
Live in Expectation of the peace, power and
prosperity that is your destiny.
Live in Expectation of you being the
achiever and receiver of all that you expect.

Dig deep into the darkness from your past. It may be the key to releasing hindrance in the present and allow progress in your future.

Let go of the things that look good in the moment, but won't leave a valuable impression once it's gone.
Let go of the things that are haunting from your past, so that it won't taint your future.

To overcome your trials, you have to

change the way in which you view them.

Don't see them as defeat,

hurtful or as a burden.

But, see them as already conquered and as

a stepping stone to your next level.

Winning "is" everything when it comes to

accomplishing the goals you

have set for your life.

Winning "is" everything when it comes to

changing your mindset toward positivity.

Winning "is" everything when it comes to

establishing your business

and business relationships.

Winning "is" everything when it comes to

building and maintaining

personal relationships.

Winning "is" everything when it

comes to obtaining success.

Winning "is" everything when you are the

winner in various aspects of your life.

Was it a loser who said winning "isn't"

everything?

Give positive, receive positive.

Speak affirmation, receive confirmation.

Think abundance, receive abundance.

Love genuinely, receive love genuinely.

Stay determined to change,

receive new life.

Seek wisdom, receive wisdom,

knowledge and understanding.

Whatever you put out, you will receive back
into your life, and more. Be careful. It is a
powerful tool and process. It works for
both positive and negative. Think twice
before you take action. Make certain your
next move will bring you a positive result.

You are unique.

You are intelligent.

You are happy.

You are valuable.

You are beautiful.

You are magnificent.

You are rich.

You are opulent.

You are prosperous.

You are successful.

Tell yourself.

Believe it yourself

and live like you are.

Take lesson in what life is teaching.
We all possess knowledge, but can always
learn and benefit from someone else's
wisdom. Sometimes, we have to learn to
keep silent and allow our minds to absorb
and process what is being said. Sometimes,
we utter words prematurely, therefore
causing our message to lose its substance.
Listen. Process. Think. Prepare. Speak.

The only way to ease your mind of clutter, is to create a mental recycle bin.

When you do mental cleaning, you are constantly getting rid of things that take up space unnecessarily.

When you practice keeping your mind clear, it makes room for the things that will move you into progress.

When you place the used and unwanted items in your mental recycle bin, remember one important thing.

You must permanently delete the items you've placed in the mental recycle bin or they will still remain on your mind.

Love is contagious.

Like the love of a child, they are so

innocently and unconditionally full of love,

you can't help but love them right back.

Love is contagious.

Your natural instinct is to adapt

to your environment.

Make your surroundings full of positive,

encouraging, wealthy, healthy,

like-minded people.

Before long you will not be adapting, you

will be functioning in what has now

become the normal.

Have you ever heard that inner voice telling
you to go ahead?

The voice that says, don't be afraid.

The voice that says, you can do it.

The voice that says, you won't fail.

The voice that says, don't
worry about them.

The voice that says, you have me.

The voice that says, exercise your faith.

The voice that says, I am your rock.

Do you listen when God is talking to you?

Remove clutter from your mind.

Remove clutter from your thoughts.

Remove clutter from your heart.

Remove clutter from your words.

Remove clutter from your friendships.

Remove clutter from your relationships.

Remove clutter from your workspace.

Remove clutter from your home.

Yes, an idol mind is the devil's workshop,

but a cluttered life is his finished project.

Accountability means to take full responsibility for your actions, with no shift of blame or accusatory mindset.

Read it again.

Are we full from the food we consume, but empty of the essential nutrients we need? Are we excellent providers for our family, but lack in giving love, time and attention? Are we gifted with multiple talents, but lack the sense of accomplishment? Are we holders of numerous college degrees, but have not mastered any of our other goals and dreams? Are we fervent readers of God's Word, but lack the wisdom and knowledge it provides? The question: Are we overfed, but undernourished?

When you feel you have failed.

When you feel defeated.

When you feel overwhelmed.

When you feel exhausted.

When you feel godforsaken.

STOP!

Change your mindset!

Now say:

I am successful. I am the victor. I am a pillar
of strength.  I am full of life.

I am a joyful warrior.  I am a child of God.

Recognize that there is a need for change.

Realize that in order to grow,

you have to let go.

Realize that only you make the

choice for your life.

Responsibility for your actions

has to be accepted.

When will you begin to live?

When will you learn of yourself to forgive?

When will you make change for your life?

When will you stop causing your own strife?

When will you let go of the past?

When will your mind be free at last?

When will you learn of yourself

to be proud?

When will you learn to proclaim it out loud?

When will you allow yourself to progress?

When will you no longer fear success?

When will you set yourself free,

and become who you were destined to be?

Give the gift of love.

It will uplift someone who is torn down.

It will shed light in a dark place.

It will bring happiness where

there is no hope.

It will open the heart of the receiver.

It will bring you joy in giving it.

Give the gift of love.

It will teach others to be unselfish.

It will renew itself in you.

It will destroy hatred.

It will change the course of your life.

It will draw you closer to God, for He is the

ultimate gift of love.

I know you challenge yourself

and the proof is in your success!

I create the words that flow from my heart

and spirit at the moment I open my eyes

every day. I hope it serves as a

breakthrough for some and a reminder to

others! Everyone does not push themselves

to move beyond their own limits, like you

and I do. But, my vision is that, if they hear

inspirational words more often,

they will be inspired to move.

Release.

Recommit.

Recourse.

Remember.

Resonate.

Restructure.

Rejuvenate.

Restore.

Retain.

Rejoice.

Reward.

Remain faithful, remain steadfast and remain unmovable in the things that you know are promised to you. Whatever is purposed for you, it is for you. No man can ever undo what God has already done! So, whether you see the promises right away or not, know that His word is as solid as a rock and will never return null or void. Remember faith, does move mountains!

Stand in the mirror and repeat after me:

How can you expect me to forgive you,

when I haven't forgiven myself?

How can you expect me to respect you,

when I don't respect myself?

How can you expect me to love you,

when I don't love myself?

You are the first priority. Fix you first.

You create the path. Forgive, respect and

love yourself and others will follow.

Then you can begin to reciprocate.

When there is love in your heart, there is peace in your home.

In order for you to become something
different, you must do something different.
In order to establish something different,
you must do something different.
In order to receive something different, you
must do something different.
In order to succeed at something different,
you must do something different.
How can you "expect" something different,
if you are not "willing"
to do something different?

True friends communicate with one
another, with words unspoken.
True friends understand one another,
with no explanation necessary.
True friends support one another,
standing side by side.
True friends believe in one another,
no questions asked.
True friends trust one another,
loyalty in place.
Are you the type of friend you want your
friend to be?

Protect your broken heart, just like any other wound. Keep it covered until it heals. Apply any healing aids, as necessary. Allow nothing to get in, open up and contaminate the wound again.

Love is not meant to be hurtful.

It is meant to bring joy and peace.

Love is not meant to be harmful.

It is meant to be healing and restoring.

Love is not meant to be deceitful.

It is meant to be honest and pure.

Love is not meant to destroy.

It is meant to build and improve.

Love is not meant to be envious.

It is meant to be content and satisfied.

Do you display love in

the way it was intended?

When you give of yourself genuinely and
unselfishly, you should naturally
expect nothing in return.

After all, it was from your heart, right?

The weight that we hold in our hearts can be so heavy, because it is what holds us to past hurt, depression, addiction, blame, bitterness, hatred, revenge, deceit, disloyalty, anger and fear.

My question: Are you willing to lose the weight, to have a healthy heart?

Who can hear you when you
haven't spoken a word?
Who can speak to your heart without
anyone else hearing it?
Who can guide you when your
feet can't seem to move?
Who can save you when you are physically,
emotionally and spiritually drowning?
Who can lift you up when you are at
your lowest point?
He's always been there.
He's never changed.
He's always reaching out to us.
He's never stopped loving us.
I know Him. You know Him.
Will you try Him?

God's love, mercy and grace, are better than any life support system man could ever create. With all of you as my witnesses, I only want my life sustained by God's life support, not a machine.

Amen.

Accept that God finishes everything started. Your faith is what determines how strongly you believe and trust in Him during the process. When you go in knowing that you've already won, there's no room for doubt, fear or defeat.

Take a moment to reflect.

How often do we tell our children we are proud of them?

We have been the builders of their confidence, strength and self-worth, from infancy until today. It doesn't matter how old they are, it still boosts them up to hear their parents say, "I'm proud of you."

Try it. You never know the effect it may have in whatever moment they are in right now.

Say 10 positive things about yourself every
day, and believe that they are true.

Do you have a vision for your life?

Is it written down?

Have you started a plan?

Will you commit to follow it through?

Are you afraid? Have you prayed?

Do you believe in what you prayed for?

Is it hard? Will you stop?

Have you failed? Will you try again?

Did you tweak the plan?

Will you try again?

Will you seek help?

Will your pride get in the way?

Will you try again?

Are you coachable?

Will you listen? Will you give up?

Do you believe in yourself?

Do you have a vision for your life?

What has not defeated you,

has made you fight harder.

What has not crippled you,

has made you walk stronger.

What has not silenced you,

has made you speak powerfully.

What has not killed you,

has made way for a second chance.

Use it wisely.

Save yourself, from yourself.

See yourself, as yourself.

Know yourself, for yourself.

Teach yourself, be yourself.

Believe yourself, in yourself.

Love yourself, by yourself.

Now, give yourself, to yourself.

Isn't that an awesome gift?

We teach our children to obey us. It saves them from harm and protects them when they listen. We feel that as parents we know what's best for them, after all they are our gifts, the jewels God entrusted us with. We would never mislead them or cause them any hurt, because we love them so unconditionally.

Do we listen to the ultimate Father, in the way we expect our children to listen to us?

Someone wants to love you, but you are not opening yourself up to receive genuine love. You keep trying to satisfy everyone, because that's how you show your love. You shower with love expecting love and appreciation in return. It doesn't work that way, and it's really an age old fight that you are not going to win, until you know the rules and play by them.

Don't be afraid of discomfort.

In order for our ancestors to pave new paths for us, it was uncomfortable, but they did it.

In order to exercise the right to vote, the fighting for new laws was uncomfortable, but they did it.

In order to drink from a segregated water fountain, the stand was uncomfortable, but they did it.

In order to ride on the front of a segregated bus, the sitting firm in that seat was uncomfortable, but she did it.

Don't be afraid of discomfort.

Stand firm in what you believe in, it changes lives for generations to come.

Review the number line from
elementary school.

Both sides of the number line go to infinity.

You can change the value on either side by

adding positive numbers to the negative

side, or adding negative numbers

to the positive side.

What value are in the number line of life?

God has never changed or forsaken us.

We transgress or fall short quit often,

but He forgives us and

loves us unconditionally.

We ask Him over and over to

reveal things to us.

We ask Him to guide us.

We ask Him to protect us.

We ask Him to answer all of our prayers.

We ask Him to bless our lives

with many things.

Because, we know He is a loving God.

We know that He will do those things for us.

The important question for us to ponder is,

what will we do for Him?

# Daily Journal

_____

_____

_____

_____

_____

_____

_____

_____

_____

_____

_____

_____

_____

_____

_____

# Daily Journal

_____

_____

_____

_____

_____

_____

_____

_____

_____

_____

_____

_____

_____

_____

## Daily Journal

_____

_____

_____

_____

_____

_____

_____

_____

_____

_____

_____

_____

_____

_____

_____

# Daily Journal

_____

_____

_____

_____

_____

_____

_____

_____

_____

_____

_____

_____

_____

## Daily Journal

_____

_____

_____

_____

_____

_____

_____

_____

_____

_____

_____

_____

_____

_____

# Daily Journal

_____

_____

_____

_____

_____

_____

_____

_____

_____

_____

_____

_____

## Daily Journal

---

---

---

---

---

---

---

---

---

---

---

---

---

# Daily Journal

_____

_____

_____

_____

_____

_____

_____

_____

_____

_____

_____

_____

## Daily Journal

_____

_____

_____

_____

_____

_____

_____

_____

_____

_____

_____

_____